D1323729

The Wee Book of
DUNDEE

Andrew Murray Scott

Black & White Publishing

First published 2003
by Black & White Publishing Ltd
99 Giles Street, Edinburgh EH6 6BZ

ISBN 1 902927 99 0

Front cover – The *Discovery, Unicorn* and Desperate Dan

Back cover – The Tay Rail Bridge, Dundee.

A full-time author, Andrew Murray Scott has spent most of his life in Dundee. He writes novels, scripts, poetry and also non-fiction, such as *Modern Dundee: Life in the City since World War Two*; *Bonnie Dundee: John Graham of Claverhouse*; *Dundee's Literary Lives, Vols 1 and II*; *The Story of Dundee* (video) and *Discovering Dundee: The Story of a City*. Further information can be found at: www.andrewmurrayscott.com

Printed and bound in Spain by Bookprint, S.L., Barcelona.

INTRODUCTION

There could be no more appropriate main cover image for this book than the Antarctic exploration ship RRS *Discovery*, built in Dundee in 1901. Starting the century in the most extreme conditions on the planet – in pack-ice at the farthest corners of the globe – she ended it floating at anchor a few hundred yards from where her story began, a major tourist attraction and celebrated worldwide. An icon of a proud city of industry, engineering and journalism, of the world capital of jute and world-famous shipbuilders – whose yards launched 600 great ships into the mighty Tay – *Discovery*'s triumphant return to her home port in 1986 heralded the city's reinvention of itself as a world centre of new technology and education, scientific exploration and cultural endeavour.

The resilience and vitality of Dundonians was severely tested in the twentieth century through hardship and war. The close-knit community spirit of the 'pletties' and suburbs like Hilltown and Lochee has now given way to a new bio-tech Citadel of Science on the Hawkhill and the lively campuses of two universities. But this evocative collection of photographs is a tribute to that earlier Dundee of the 'wahshies', city arcade, trams and the old swimming baths. These haunting photographs take us into the foyer of Green's Playhouse and the Vic cinema, let us linger again at the old Overgate, on the forecourt of West Station, at the top of the Wellgate Steps and in front of D. M. Brown's. We are reminded of the fame and glory of the city's sporting heroes and of crowds turning out for visits by royalty; summer days when Broughty beach was busier than Benidorm, when folk queued at the bus stances of Shore Terrace or for a ticket on the 'Fifies'. Each one of these magnificent pictures of Dundee in the past century has been carefully selected from the vast archive of D. C. Thomson & Co. Ltd to inspire recollections and help celebrate the life and times of one of Scotland's greatest and most versatile cities.

Andrew Murray Scott

A water-cart in August 1932, used to spray the streets to keep the dust down and help dissipate horse dung. Children often formed a procession behind these carts – having removed their socks and shoes – to enjoy the jets of cold water on their feet. One child would spot the water-cart and shout 'Scooty-boy, hoy!' and dozens of others would appear. Horse-drawn cleansing carts leading processions of barefoot children remained a common sight until the mid-1930s, when the carts were replaced.

Frank Russell's bookshop at 26 Barrack Street was established in 1915 and remained there until 1962, when it moved to 130 Nethergate and then on to 95 Nethergate. Frank Russell himself died in 1959, by which time the business was long-established as the premier bookshop of Dundee. In 1979 the premises became known as the University Bookshop and, in 1995, the shop was acquired by Blackwell's, finally closing as a bookshop in 1999 when it became a hair salon. This photograph of the Barrack Street premises was taken in about 1930 and shows the queues outside the shop before school term started; in those days pupils were expected to provide their own books, and there was a thriving business in second-hand textbooks.

The Dundee Book Store
School & College
TEXT BOOKS
New & Second-Hand

Dundonians admire the new tram on 5 November 1930 as it passes the spectacular Old Town House, which was doomed to be demolished in 1931 to make way for the new City Square. Much-loved by Dundonians as a meeting place, 'the Pillars', designed by William Adam in 1731, was regarded as the most elegant and impressive town house in Scotland. The building was a symbol of the confidence and ambition of eighteenth-century Dundee and its demolition was an unpardonable act of municipal vandalism. Birrell Ltd Confectioners can be seen at 26 High Street, on the approximate site of the present-day bookshop, Ottakar's.

The King's Theatre & Hippodrome in about 1925, when it was hosting prestigious opera companies such as D'Oyly Carte, as well as variety acts and shows by music-hall stars such as Harry Lauder, Will Fyffe and Marie Lloyd. Later it would host concerts by pop singers such as Cliff Richard.

In its heyday the opulence of its interior and its comfortable furnishings were widely famed. Opening in 1909, it began to double-up as a cinema in 1928 and was renamed the Gaumont in 1950 and later the Odeon, before its closure in June 1981. It reopened as a theme bar and restaurant in May 1998 and is now the Deja Vu nightclub.

The Howff is the walled heart of medieval Dundee,
offering today, as ever, an opportunity to meditate amid
the bustle of the city, or read the fascinating inscriptions
on the ancient gravestones:

Away, vain world! thou ocean of annoyes
And com sweet heaven, with thy eternal joyes. (1639)

The garden lands of the Grey Friars' convent were gifted
to the town in 1564 for use as a graveyard, and many
of the sepulchres are of great historical interest,
including the grave of the notorious Provost Riddoch at
the north-eastern corner which, as one commentator
wryly noted, 'has its back to the wall'! This unusual
photograph dates from 1936. Note the factory
chimney of the extensive Tay works and also that there
is no Courier tower extension – added in 1960 – to
block the view of the Law.

*The Vic started life as a dance hall and music hall and,
in 1903, became the Gaiety Theatre, hosting shows by
well-known vaudeville stars. In 1915 it succumbed to
the cinema craze and was renamed the Victoria Palace,
but from 1933 – the date of this photograph – it came
under the ownership of J. B. Milne and continued to
host occasional circus acts, despite the fact that Milne's
expensive Riley was once sat on by a visiting elephant!
A later manager, the tireless Bill Ramsay, kept the Vic
operating long after all other early cinemas had given up
the ghost and it closed in September 1990, the second-
longest-surviving cinema in Scotland (after the Salon in
Glasgow). It had been a great favourite of jute workers
from nearby mills and had also been highly regarded
because of its 'chummy' – or double – seats at the back
which allowed courting rituals to take place!*

Opened by a twenty-four-year-old Lochee man, David Miller Brown, in 1908, D. M. Brown's became famous for its American-inspired opulent interior of glass, carved mahogany and marble which, in the opinion of the Dundee Advertiser, *'excels anything of the kind in Scotland, if indeed it is equalled by anything in Britain'. Beginning its long life as a single-fronted 'Hosier & Glover' at 80 High Street where three assistants sold 'smallwares, trimmings and underclothing', it had developed a staff of 400 by Brown's death in 1934, when this picture was taken. By then it was a general drapers with a much-patronised tea-room and 400-foot-long haberdashery arcade. Acquired by House of Fraser in 1952, and renamed Arnotts in 1972, it survived until closure in 2002.*

The Duke and Duchess of York at the opening of Fleming Gardens Housing Scheme in 1933. Twenty-one acres of land had been gifted to the city by one of Dundee's greatest benefactors, the financier Robert Fleming, in order to combat the slum problem, and this led to 496 houses being built to the south of Clepington Road between 1929 and 1933. The eighty-four-year-old Fleming – father of the explorer, Peter, and the writer, Ian, and seen here talking with Duchess Elizabeth – was awarded the Freedom of the City on the same day.

King George VI and Queen Elizabeth talking to workers at Caledon Shipyard on 10 March 1941. The shipyard operated around the clock to produce vessels for the war effort and the workforce included women employed as welders, taken on, as in the First World War, because of the shortage of male workers. The monarch spent some three-and-a-half hours in the city, also touring Ashton Jute Works, the Blackness Foundry and naval units at the docks, and the visit was a great morale booster, some 20,000 cramming into the centre to watch the royals arrive at the City Chambers for afternoon tea with local dignitaries.

The Food Office and National Registration Office at Long Wynd in 1945. A few years earlier in 1941, the famous writer Edwin Muir had worked in this office, where clerical work associated with rationing was undertaken and where Dundonians were issued with their ration-cards and coupons. Rationing was at first resisted by some sections of the population – there was a thriving black market – but soon covered all foodstuffs and most materials. Clothes rationing was not abolished until March 1949 and identity cards remained in use until February 1952, although meat coupons were used until July 1954. Most unpopular of all, however, was bread rationing, which was introduced for the first time in 1950 – by a Dundee MP, John Strachey, in his role as Food Minister – and contributed to the defeat of the Labour governments in 1950 and 1951.

24

Prefabs first appeared in Dundee in 1943 at Seabraes and many more were built at various locations, including Douglas and Angus, Camperdown, Mains of Fintry and here at Blackshade. This photograph shows the prefabs still going strong 20 years later in July 1965 and at that time there were still 678 in use in the city. Not bad for 'temporary' housing! What tenants most liked about them – and I speak from experience – was that they were detached. Each family had a home of their own, with their own front and back doors and garden space, which many used for growing vegetables.

The buster stall at Mid Kirk Style in the old Overgate in August 1949. A lady, possibly Mrs De Gernier, ladles out a 'buster' – mushy peas on pale flabby chips with a dash of vinegar and salt. The popular snack cost tuppence for a bowl's worth – for a penny, you got the same on a smaller plate – and you ate the delicacy with a spoon, sitting on a wooden bench under the makeshift tarpaulin shelter. With only rudimentary hygiene facilities – spoons were dipped in soapy water before being reused, a fact which rarely seemed to attract comment at the time – they were a feature of Dundee life which came to an end before the advent of the EC Food Regulation Commission, who would undoubtedly have had the buster stalls closed down immediately!

Panoramic view of a frosty Dundee harbour from a window of Mather's Hotel at the junction of Whitehall Crescent and South Union Street in January 1949. West Dock Street is in the immediate foreground, and in the Earl Grey Dock navy vessels can be seen among smaller craft. The Royal Arch almost hides the entrance forecourt of the Empress Ballroom and, to the right of it, the tidal harbour is in the middle distance. Beyond them can be seen the King William IV dock, then the Victoria dock and, in the distance, the Camperdown dock. Steam can also be seen from East Station, which is just out of shot on the left, as well as from another train which is heading east to Broughty Ferry.

West Station in April 1957, from the junction of Yeaman Shore and Union Street looking down South Union Street to the 'Fifies' booking-office and Craig Pier. Dock Street is on the left and there is a police box on the central island. Built for the Caledonian Railway Company, the red-towered sandstone station was demolished in May 1966 – despite widespread opposition – just one year after the last train puffed away from the platform, heading west for Glasgow.

This photograph was taken further down South Union Street on the same day in 1957 and shows cars and lorries queuing for the Tay Ferry to take them over the river to Newport-on-Tay. On the left is Craig Street and on the right, Taybridge Station, built in 1958, no part of which survives in the modern station of the same name. Beyond the glass-fronted ferry booking-office on the right are Paladini's garage and car showroom, public toilets and the eastern end of Riverside Drive.

Trams in Lochee High Street in the 1950s. Note the East Church, demolished in 1960.

The Queen at the centenary of Dundee Royal Infirmary in June 1955. Prince Philip, who is followed by Lord Provost William Hughes, clearly has an eye for the nurses!

We're having a heatwave! It was 73°F in the shade at 5 p.m. on Broughty beach on Saturday, 8 August 1958. It was also the first day of the new football season and 21,000 fans sweltered in the full glare of the sun at Dens Park. The local paper reported that 'practically every man had his jacket off and women wore flimsy summer dresses. Thousands put on sunglasses.' Despite this, three men and five women fainted before full-time. Since only four trams were operating due to stoppage of overtime, huge queues built up for buses to the beach and, in the evening, it was even worse.

By 7.30 p.m. huge queues had built up at the No. 6 terminus in Broughty Ferry and it was well after 9 p.m. before they were cleared.

The winter of 1958 brought some of the worst weather conditions since 1947 and on 8 February all roads around the city were blocked. Coal lorries were abandoned in snowdrifts in Fintry, and both Dundee MP George Thomson and Sir Garnet Wilson were among those who spent twenty-two hours trapped on a snowbound train en route for Dundee.

Thirty people were injured in accidents in the city and shops were deserted, but this policeman manages to keep the traffic moving at the junction of Union Street and Nethergate during the blizzard.

Evocative view of the High Street and Overgate in April 1959. In January 1961 the demolition would begin to make way for the new Overgate centre. The central block in the photograph – known as 'General Monck's lodging' and dating from the fifteenth century – was one of the first buildings to fall to the bulldozers. Note the stair tower, railed-in at the top, which was once a common feature of Dundee 'lands'. Many popular shops, including The Sixty Minute Cleaners, The Washington Café, Wilson's Bonanza Stores, Meltoy, Christies the Drapers, the Kinnear restaurant, the Dundee Eastern Co-operative Society, and small businesses like hairdressers, fishmongers and vehicle hirers were to disappear. The digging also disturbed hundreds of jumbled skeletons and skulls in the mass graves left after General Monck's sack of the city in 1651.

Another panoramic view, this time east along Dock Street in the early 1960s and again showing the Earl Grey Dock, the Royal Arch and the popular Shore Terrace bus stances. While most Dundonians believed that direct contact between the city centre and the river and its harbour activities made for a more interesting and vibrant city, that was to change in 1966 with the decision to bring the new road bridge right into the heart of the city. The dock was filled in to provide new access roads, the Royal Arch was demolished, bus services were re-routed and the drab multi-storey Tayside House was erected. Thereafter pedestrians struggled to reach the river by a network of elevated walkways over busy traffic lanes.

Women sharing a joke at the 'wahshie', or public wash-house, at Caldrum Street in March 1958. The Caldrum Street wash-house was built in 1902 after the runaway success of the first one which opened in Guthrie Street in 1898, and its success was put down to its site 'in a part of the city inhabited by the better class of working people'.

Open from 6 a.m. to 6 p.m., laundry was often transported to these 'wahshies' – described as 'caverns of steam' beneficial for the complexion – in tin baths or wicker baskets mounted on folding push-chairs. They also catered for bathers and, although the number of annual washes declined slightly from 46,000 in 1909 to 44,000 in 1959, the number of bathers doubled from 12,000 to 24,000 over the same period.

Looking down the Hilltown across Victoria Road to the Wellgate in July 1953. In the foreground are the public lavatories and phone box. The Wellgate Steps which descended from the south side of Victoria Road were a popular rendezvous, and the narrow streets of the Wellgate area – bounded by Victoria Road, the Cowgate and Meadowside – was a good area for bargains, with butchers, bakers, fruiterers, furniture shops, a TV and radio specialist and music shops. During my school lunch-hours I used to visit an amusement arcade there which had, on its first floor, a large go-karting track – or it might have been Dodgems. The massive six-storey Wellgate Centre took several years to complete and opened in 1976, covering over all of the area and featuring a three-level shopping complex.

The Hub kiosk in the High Street sold newspapers and cigarettes – often in singles – from 6 a.m. to midnight and was a feature of the city centre from 1910. In 1932 William Young sold it to Bob Lamb, who ran it for nearly thirty years until 1960, when he retired aged seventy-five. This photograph was taken on 20 July, his last day. Squeezed into the space of a former stairwell between H. Samuel, the jewellers, and Timpson's shoeshop and measuring only three square feet, it was reputed to be the smallest shop in the world. After it closed down, the kiosk was integrated into the façade of H. Samuel.

The continuing occurrence of minor accidents at Dundee jute mills led to the formation of the Accident Prevention League and here, at the Camperdown works, mill workers study the 'league table' for the month of August 1957. The jute industry was at that time still employing 18,000 people in the city and had begun to diversify into polypropylene products and tufted carpet backing. Four years earlier the industry had received a massive boost after wide-scale flooding led to overtime working to produce nearly 24 million sandbags and, in 1956, Dundee's jute workers got Christmas Day as a holiday for the first time – as well as two days at New Year. The industry was in gradual decline, however, and, after 170 years of jute, the last mill, Tay Spinners, closed in 1998.

accident prevention league

AUG 1957

ACCIDENTS

LEAGUE EFFICIENCY	WORKS	THIS MONTH	LAST MONTH	TOTAL TO DATE
1	RASHIEWELL	0	0	0
2	WALTON	0	0	3
3	HEATHFIELD	0	0	1
4	STANLEY	0	0	5
5	TAY CALENDER	1	0	2
6	TAY CARPETS	0	0	7
7	VICTORIA (FORFAR)	1	1	4
8	BOW BRIDGE	0	2	23
9	ANGUS	1	0	5
10	MANHATTAN	3	1	17
11	MAXWELLTOWN	1	0	4
12	CALDRUM	3	1	23
	CAMPERDOWN	3	3	33
	DOUGLASFIELD	1	0	6
15	LONGTOWN	1	0	13

A view from Broughty Ferry Road taken in August 1979 in the last months of the shipyard's existence. Nearly 600 great ships – giant tankers, Blue Star liners, Empire cargo ships, ferries and aircraft-carriers – had slid down the slipways into the Tay since 1874 but, after a battle against the tide of international competition, nationalisation and falling demand, Dundee's shipbuilding days were over. A determined but unsuccessful sit-in by 140 men drew public attention to the final assassination of the yard, which had been struggling for survival since the early 1960s. A hundred years of clanging hammers, riveters and welders' arc-lights were over.

Bandleader Andy Lothian Sr, seen here with his twelve-piece band at the Palais in November 1955, was a familiar sight for generations of Dundonians who went to 'the jigging' at least one night a week. Some of the biggest names in entertainment performed here and the music was livened up by regular vocalists such as Charlie Coats. They were hired after singing on guest nights – a hard apprenticeship among highly discerning audiences – and were expected to perform all the up-to-date chart hits, singing seven nights a week with two afternoon sessions.

Bobby Cannon, the nineteen-year-old trainee hotel manager from Pitlochry, twisted non-stop for ninety-four hours and fifty minutes to win £105 in the J. M. Ballroom's marathon twisting contest in March 1962. Nearly 40 competitors took part and 20,000 members of the public came in to watch over the four days of the event. This photograph was taken several weeks later when Bobby returned to Dundee to perform an 'exhibition' show to celebrate his success. The J. M., under 'Murdie' Wallace, held out against modernity until 1959, when jiving was finally permitted on the dance floor and rock-and-roll – in moderation – was allowed, although strict codes of dress and behaviour were still maintained and Teddy boys were not admitted.

Dancing has long been a Dundee passion and here, in November 1962, at Hungry Mary's – the ballroom of the Craigtay Hotel, otherwise known as The Hubara – the foxtrot was popular. Although the wartime boom for dancing was over, there were still many venues in the city, including the J. M. Ballroom, the Palais, the West End Palais, the Rendezvous, the Tay Hotel, Queen's Hotel, Star Ballroom, the Empress Ballroom, the Progress Dance Hall and many more. But these were soon to be overtaken by the new discotheques, which attracted larger numbers of a mainly younger generation and began to supersede the more formal dances, leading to a new boom in Dundee dancing.

Johnny Hudson and the Hi-Four play for spectators during a break in a twisting marathon at the West End Palais ('Robies') in Well Street, Hawkhill, on 3 March 1964. The twister requiring attention is John Faulds, possessor of a fine pair of baseball boots, and the Dundee High schoolboy is the son of the owner, Ron Duncan. Hudson's real name was Johnny Moran and his own band, Johnny Hudson and the Teen Beats, had played on the same bill as The Beatles at the Caird Hall in 1963. However, he left them to join the Dundee super-group on the eve of their departure for a residency booking in Hamburg that same year.

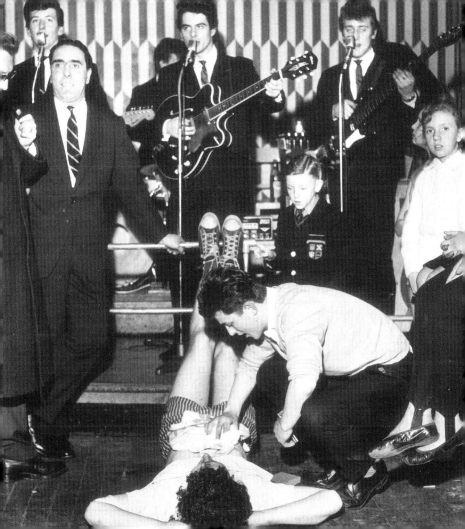

The main entrance of Dundee Repertory Theatre, Nicoll Street, in August 1958. The Rep had been based in the old Forester's Hall since 1939, the year of its formation. However, after a fire in 1963, the theatre company was forced to move into temporary accommodation – including, for a brief period, a tent in Camperdown Park and then St Columba's church in Lochee Road – before moving to its custom-built premises in Tay Square on 8 April 1982. The Rep is now in the premier league of national drama venues and hosts the only full-time ensemble company of actors in Scotland.

The old saltwater swimming baths hold particularly fond memories for many Dundonians. Watery noises echoed around the tiled walls of the men's pool, ladies' pool and larger gala pool, and sunlight was cast across the water from high windows and the glass roof. The narrow entrance from the south side at West Protection Wall, with its small foyer, ticket office and turnstiles, led you into either the 'ponds' or up to the tiered spectators' balcony – on three sides of the gala pool. There were also Turkish baths, separate bath cubicles and a café where you could buy a 'shivery bite'. Note the striped awnings above the cubicle doors – a feature of the mixed-bathing gala pool only. This photograph of the Harris Academy Gala on 16 March 1962 brings back the excitement and fun of the old baths.

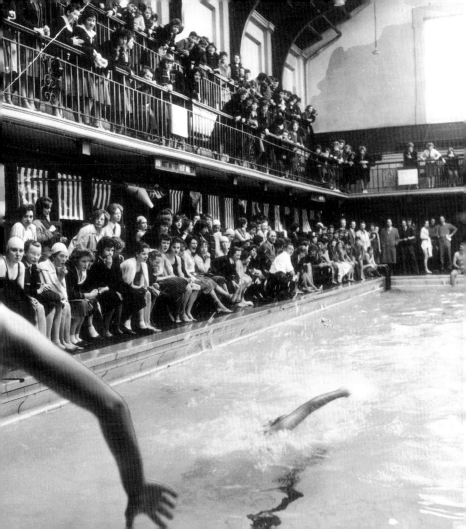

The high diving-boards at the gala pool in the old baths afforded young men an excellent opportunity to show off their skills in front of an audience. This photograph was taken in 1965 from the highest of the two diving-boards.

In April 1973 the baths were replaced by the new Olympia Leisure Centre which was built next door and *which was later to be described by American writer Paul Theroux as 'having the look of a Russian interrogation headquarters, a vast drab Lubyanka in rain-streaked concrete'. Despite their external appearance, the excellent facilities include giant flumes, water cannon, wild water and wave machines, as well as a fitness suite and, of course, swimming pools!*

Green's Playhouse was the most luxurious of Dundee's twenty-eight cinemas. It seated 4117 and had a restaurant catering for 160 which could be extended into the foyer on busy nights. The decor was fully in tune with the glamour of the cinema age and its most distinguishing external feature was the stylish finned metal advertising tower, lit in neon with a squint 'U'. It also hosted beauty contests and shows by such stars as Bob Hope. Green's is now Mecca Bingo, Britain's busiest bingo venue, with a membership of 15,000 and average weekly attendances of 11,000.

The Pavilion, Baxter Park, in May 1958. The Renaissance-style building divides the formal upper part of the park from the grassed lower space and tennis courts. Gifted by jute baron David Baxter, the thirty-eight-acre park was formally opened in 1863 in a lavish ceremony attended by Prime Minister Lord Russell and 70,000 spectators. A marble bust of the benefactor has since been removed to the McManus Galleries and the pavilion itself, which endured decades of neglect and vandalism, is presently undergoing lottery-funded restoration. In 1958 part of the pavilion was in use as Forino's Café and also sold ice creams and sweets. In the 1970s, popular outdoor concerts were held in the park, which now hosts spectacular annual firework displays on Guy Fawkes' night.

W. Alexander & Sons' Bus Station at Trades Lane in the Seagate in October 1959. Each bus was staffed by a driver and a conductor with a metal ticket-punching machine belted across his chest. The blue-and-yellow coach fleet, with its distinctive bluebird logo, covered all the country areas of Angus, Fife and Perthshire and as far afield as Aberdeen, Glasgow, Edinburgh, Blackpool and London. The nearest stance, No. 6, covered the Forfar via Letham route, calling at Baldovie Toll, Murroes, Wellbank, Luckyslap and Monikie.

lyde, one of the last working horses in Dundee, prepares to draw his final load for Robert Adam, haulage contractor of Malcolm Street, in January 1966, although another horse, called Paddy, was still working in 1969. In the early years of the century Clydesdales were the life-blood of the city, delivering all kinds of loads. They carried water, as well as meat – covered with tarpaulins – from the slaughterhouses, moved sand, stone, jute bales and flour around the docks, shifted stage scenery from the theatres, and even moved railway wagons. Six or eight horses in harness could also transport steel beams for engineering purposes such as the building of West Station. But while a pair of horses could carry between three and three and a half tons, a new motorised lorry in the early 1930s could carry six tons with ease and so the days of horses were numbered.

Wish you were here? Monday, 23 July 1962 and the start of the holiday fortnight. The weekend had seen downpours and thunder and lightning, none of which had prevented 30,000 Dundonians from setting off on their travels. Eight relief trains were laid on to cope with the 'holiday fever' on the first Saturday, the main destinations being Aberdeen and Glasgow, and seven more relief trains were ordered for the day after. The Courier's *editorial warned of the danger of road accidents with such a frenzied exodus and urged motorists to be patient. In the event there were only three crashes in the mist and rain of Saturday and everyone involved escaped with minor cuts and bruises.*

Equally lucky were the passengers on a holiday excursion train to Inverness, which scraped the diesel engine of a south-bound train near Pitlochry. Taxi companies were inundated with fifty requests per hour: one family hired a taxi to take them to Ayr, at a cost of ten guineas, and another to Deeside! In 66°F heat, however, there was absolutely nothing wrong with Broughty beach – and these folk would agree.

The enthusiasm for ice cream among Dundee kids is evident from this photograph taken at one of the beach kiosks on the same day, 23 July 1962. Two of the boys seem to have committed the fashion faux pas of wearing the same shirt! Or maybe they were brothers? Although the kiosks carried an extensive range of confectionery, the most popular choices were still the 'sliders', the 99s and – for the penny-pinchers – the cones which, in 1962, cost all of a ha'penny!

St Mary's RC Church, Forebank, looking down Forebank Street to the river in August 1970. Built in 1851 on a two-acre site to accommodate almost 2000 worshippers, the Romanesque church with its twin campaniles – and the occasional sight of a priest or two entering or exiting – always seemed too exotic for a Dundee backstreet, as if it had somehow been borrowed from a remote Eastern European town. Monks of the Marist order founded an evening school here in 1860 and in 1863 a school for boys, and the Marist brothers still have links with Our Lady's RC primary school in nearby Ann Street.

Cathie McCabe's record and fancy goods shop in the City Arcade in 1971. The Arcade, founded in the 1920s, proved to be one of the city's busiest shopping centres well into the 1970s. With its unique octagonal counters to display LPs and tapes, Cathie McCabe's was situated opposite the Choc Box confectioners and Hynd's Amusements stall – with its one-arm bandits, fruit-machines and automatic rides, including the wooden horse which bucked to the tune of 'Champion the Wonder Horse'.

Boxer Dick McTaggart showing the Val Barker trophy for best Olympic stylist in 1956 to his father, mother and grandmother at the family home in Dens Road on 13 December. Twelve days earlier at the Melbourne Games, McTaggart defeated West Germany's Harry Kurschat to take the Olympic Lightweight Championship. McTaggart won a bronze medal in the 1960 Olympics in Rome and he also won five ABA titles, not to mention gold medals at the Cardiff Commonwealth Games in 1958 and the European Championships in 1961 in Belgrade. In his 634 contests, he was only once knocked out and lost – or, as he put it, 'was robbed' – just twenty-four times. His only injuries during his career were a cut eye and a thick ear and he put his success down to being fast on his feet. He refused to turn professional and instead coached the Scottish Amateur International side.

Dundee FC line up against FC Cologne at Dens Park on 6 September 1962. Bob Shankly's legendary – and home-grown – team had conquered all opposition to win the League championship for the first time in 1961–2 and, in their European run, they would beat the Germans 8–1.

Dundee United players do a lap of honour after their brave 1–1 performance against IFK Gothenburg on 20 May 1987 in the second leg of the UEFA Cup final at Tannadice. Watched by a worldwide TV audience of 70 million, they lost out due to a 0–1 defeat in the first leg. But manager Jim McLean declared that his players 'gave every ounce they had', and the capacity crowd stayed behind to applaud the only Scottish team ever to reach the final of the UEFA Cup – a staggering performance from a club which, until 1983, had not won a single trophy.

Liz Lynch with her father and mother after winning Commonwealth Gold in the 10,000 metres in 1986. As Liz McColgan, she is Dundee's greatest-ever athlete, winning silver at the Seoul Olympics in 1988 and gold at the World Championships in 1990 – 'the greatest performance by a British athlete in the history of long-distance running', according to Brendan Foster at the time. Liz won the New York marathon at her first attempt in 1991 and the London marathon twice, in 1991 and 1996. BBC Sports Personality of the Year in 1991, Liz received her red book from Michael Aspel in the Caird Hall on This Is Your Life *in 1992 at the age of only twenty-eight and was the subject of a biography in the same year. In 2003 she was awarded an honorary doctorate from Abertay University in recognition of her achievements and role as a sporting ambassador.*

Scotland's greatest twentieth-century landscape painter,
Dr James McIntosh Patrick, and the view from his
studio window. Citizen of the Year in 1979 and the
recipient of an OBE and numerous honorary doctorates,
Patrick died in 1998 aged ninety-one. Apart from his
years as an art student at Glasgow School of Art and
service in the Camouflage Corps in North Africa during
the Second World War, he retained a lifelong association
with Dundee, working part-time for Valentines and as a
lecturer at Duncan of Jordanstone College of Art. His
distinctive landscapes of his favourite locations in
Angus and Perthshire continue to be admired worldwide,
and many local artists remember his art tutorial classes
with great affection.

And the band played on! In this instance, the Montrose Academy Band on 23 June 1991 in the cast-iron Magdalen Green bandstand, saved after four years' effort by the local community council which raised funds to have it restored. Dr James McIntosh Patrick contributed a painting to be auctioned by the campaign. The listed monument is the centrepiece of the open space which has seen some of Dundee's most dramatic moments, including great demonstrations for reform and scenes of unrest in previous times, as well as a wide variety of sporting and leisure pursuits. Cricket was often played there in the last decade of the nineteenth century and today, with its proximity and view of the river and the rail bridge, it remains one of the most enchanting open spaces in the city.

The £20m Wellcome Trust building in Hawkhill – where 240 scientists battle the causes of cancer, malaria, sleeping sickness, diabetes and hereditary eczema – part of Dundee's Citadel of Science, a world centre of bio-medical research. It would be fitting if it were to be in the home port of Captain Scott's Antarctic research ship Discovery, moored since 1986 in a custom-built dock at the riverfront, that a cure for these terrible diseases was discovered.